BATS!

THE ONLY FLYING MAMMALS

Bats for Kids

Children's Mammal Books

BABY PROFESSOR
EDUCATION KIDS

Speedy Publishing LLC

40 E. Main St. #1156

Newark, DE 19711

www.speedypublishing.com

Copyright 2017

In this book, we're going to talk about bats. So, let's get right to it!

Lots of people are scared of bats. They're afraid because bats have been portrayed as bloodsuckers. There are a few types of bats that consume blood, but it's very rare for them to get blood from humans.

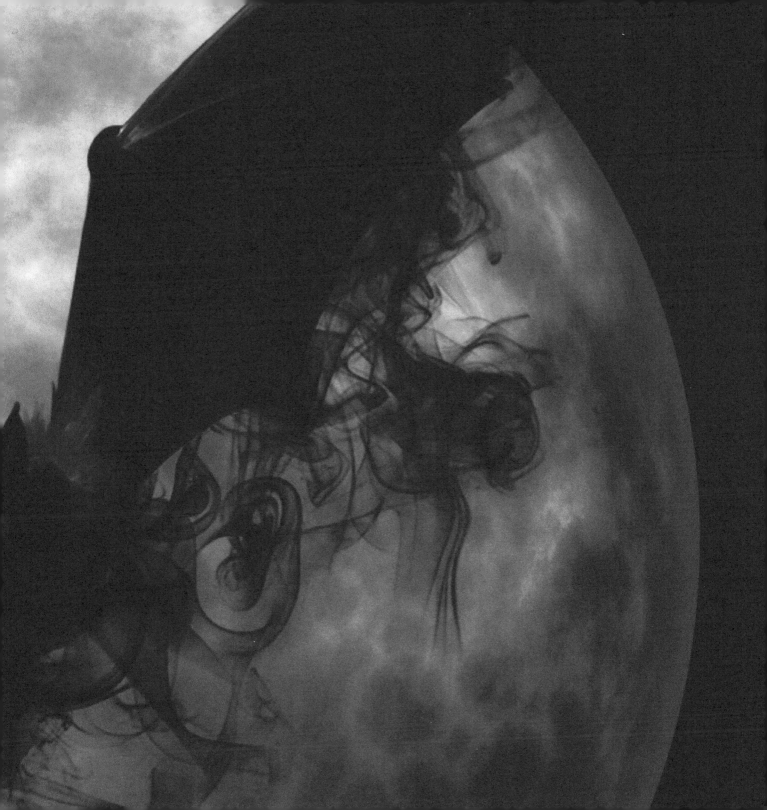

Those that do lick blood get it from cattle and other animals. Many people are worried that they'll get rabies from bats.

Bats do sometimes carry rabies but that doesn't happen very often either. Only about 5-6% of bats carry rabies.

BATS ARE SMALLER THAN ONE GENERALLY THINKS

The truth is that most bats are actually very beneficial to humans because they eat insects that destroy crops, such as June bugs, or insects that carry disease, such as mosquitoes.

SOUTHERN BENT-WING BAT

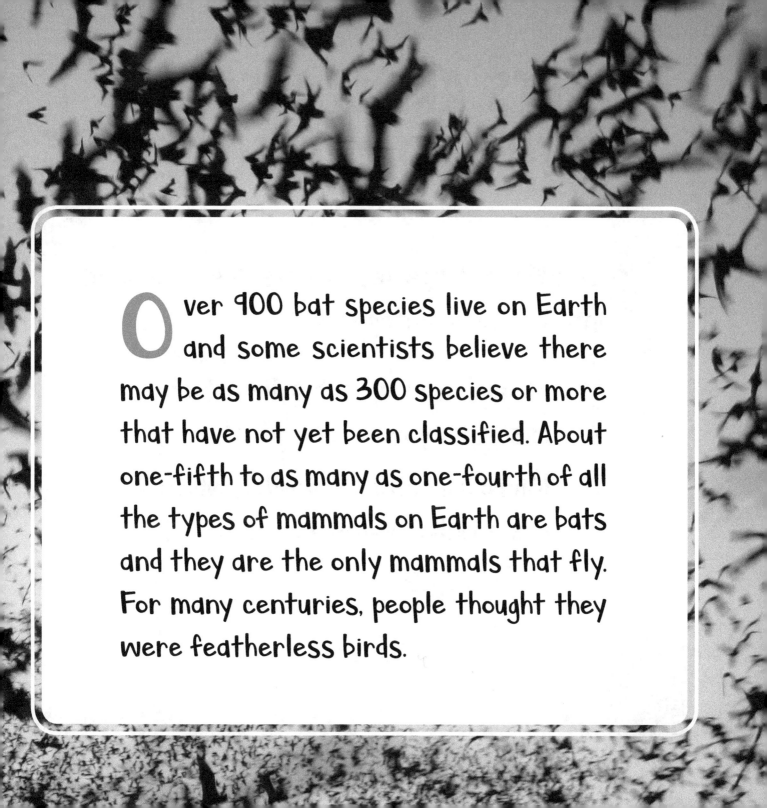

Over 900 bat species live on Earth and some scientists believe there may be as many as 300 species or more that have not yet been classified. About one-fifth to as many as one-fourth of all the types of mammals on Earth are bats and they are the only mammals that fly. For many centuries, people thought they were featherless birds.

BATS ARE CLASSIFIED INTO TWO CATEGORIES

The different species of bats are organized into two main categories.

* Megachiroptera suborder, which essentially means megabats

* Microchiroptera suborder, which essentially means microbats

The word "chiroptera" means winged hands. In fact, when bats fly, they are basically flapping their hands.

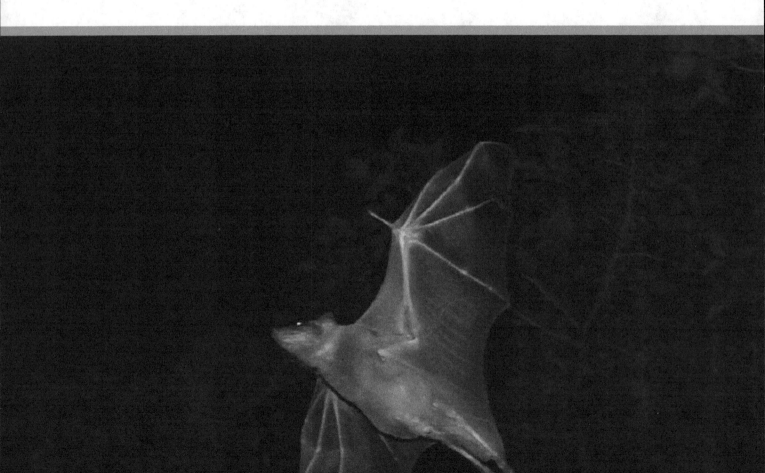

Generally, the megabats, such as flying foxes, have bigger wingspans and body sizes than the microbats. However, this isn't universally true. There are some microbat species that are larger than some megabat species.

GREY HEADED FLYING FOX

WHAT ARE THE LARGEST AND SMALLEST MEGABATS?

Flying foxes are the largest of the species of megabats. Some flying foxes have 6-foot wingspans and they can weigh over 2 pounds, which is very lightweight for their size. Weighing only half an ounce, the fruit bat with the scientific name Macroglossus minimus has a long tongue, but only has a 10-inch wingspan. It is one of the smallest of the megabats.

WHAT ARE THE LARGEST AND SMALLEST MICROBATS?

The false vampire bat, also called the spectral bat, is the largest of the microbat species. Its wingspan can get to a size of 40 inches across and it weighs a little over 6 ounces.

SPECTRAL BAT

The smallest bat, which is also the smallest mammal on Earth, is the tiny bumblebee bat. Its size is about 1.25 inches in length and it only weighs about 0.07 ounces, the same weight as some hummingbirds.

KITTI'S HOG-NOSED BAT STUFFED SPECIMEN

ARCTIC

WHERE DO BATS LIVE?

Bats live almost everywhere in the world, except for the tundra of the Arctic and Antarctica and a few isolated islands. They can be found in almost every different type of habitat from mountainous regions, to farmlands and forests, and even in tropical rainforests. Some have learned how to thrive in city areas as well.

They prefer warmer locations close to the equator, however, they have strategies for surviving colder temperatures. Like birds, some migrate to warmer areas when the temperatures drop. Others go into an unusual state of hibernation that lasts less time than most animal hibernations.

LESSER SHORT-NOSED FRUIT BAT

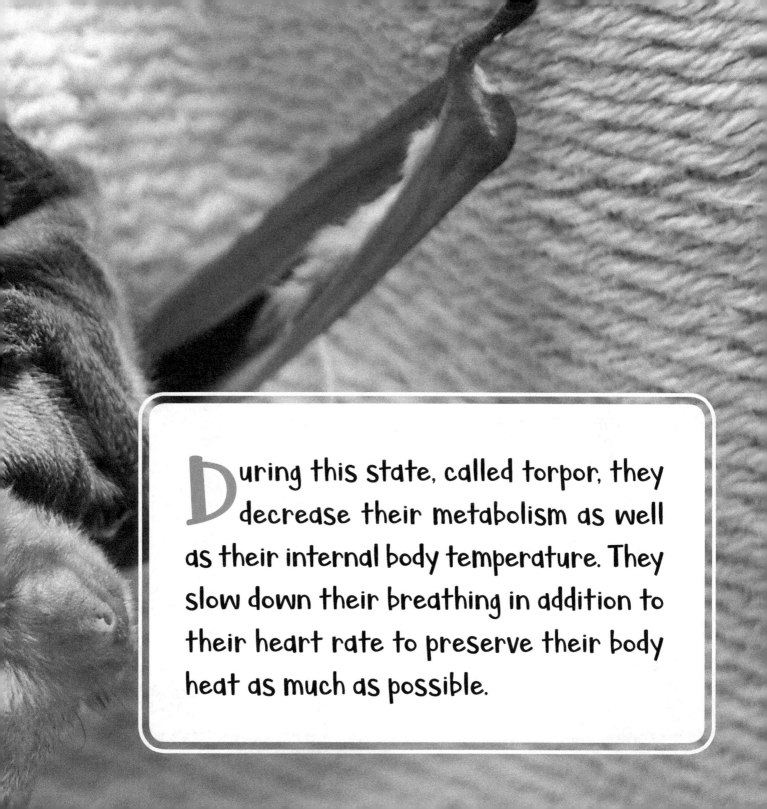

During this state, called torpor, they decrease their metabolism as well as their internal body temperature. They slow down their breathing in addition to their heart rate to preserve their body heat as much as possible.

Although bats can sit upright, they rarely do. They roost in mines, caves, trees, and barns and they generally hang upside down from tree limbs, rafters, or the ceilings of caves by using their very sharp claws. They congregate in large groups in these places in order to get shelter from the weather, fend off predators, and give birth to and nurture their young.

These large groups, called colonies, generally have at least 100 bats and up to 1,000 bats.

The largest colony of bats in the world live in Bracken Cave outside of San Antonio, Texas. Over 20 million bats are estimated to live there!

MEXICAN FREE-TAILED BATS EXITING BRACKEN BAT CAVE

Bats sleep during the daytime and then emerge from their shelters to hunt at night. This means they are nocturnal. They may fly over 30 miles to seek their favorite hunting grounds at night.

NGEZI FOREST-BATS

WHAT DO BATS EAT?

Bats have a varied diet. Depending on the species, they eat fruit and flowers. They also eat nectar, leaves, and pollen. Some bats like fruit juice and will squeeze fruits in their mouths to drink the juice.

BABY EASTERN RED BAT

Many eat small insects and a few lick spoonful-sized amounts of blood.

Megabats are generally fruit eaters and microbats are insectivores, which means they eat insects.

SEBAS SHORT-TAILED FRUIT BAT

MALAY FLYING FOX

The megabat described as the Malayan flying fox, which eats fruit, can eat about 50% of its body weight daily. The brown bat, a type of microbat, is very beneficial to humans since it can consume more than 1,000 small insects like mosquitoes in just one hour!

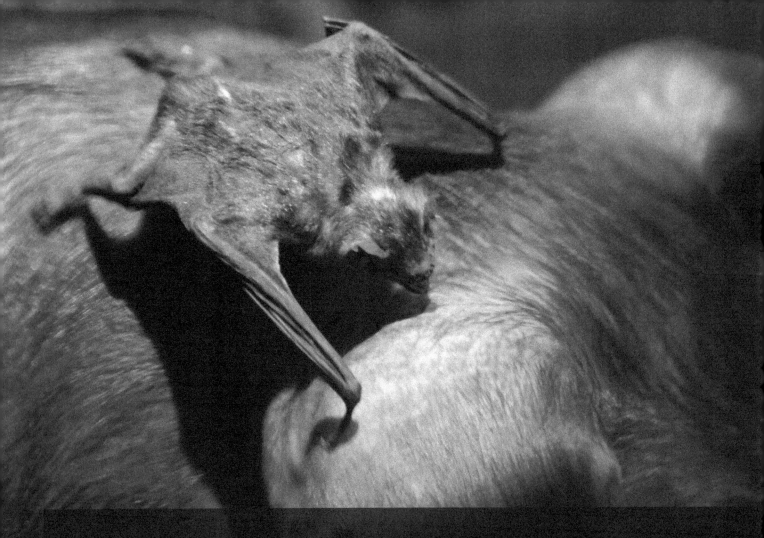

Vampire bats do consume blood, but rarely from humans. They creep quietly on the ground to attack cattle and deer. They make a cut that is V-shaped in the animals hide and then lick the blood.

Sometimes the animals remain asleep while they do it. They don't really suck blood like they do in vampire stories.

They can consume twice their weight in blood every day. The vampire bats have a special substance in their saliva that makes their victims' blood flow. It's an anticoagulant and is being used to help human patients that have had strokes or heart disease because it helps their blood flow more easily within their bodies.

THE MATING HABITS OF BATS

Bats have some interesting mating behaviors that other animals don't have. When they are ready to mate they get together in places where they generally hibernate. They have a "swarming event," which takes place in either the late summer or the first part of the fall. Enormous numbers of them fly at the same time. They chase after each other and do amazing aerial acrobatics.

BATS HIBERNATING

It's not clear how the females select their mates, but scientists believe that the males that perform the best aerial stunts and are the most agile are seen as the most desirable mates. Once a female and male get together, they go to an isolated place in the cave or other shelter to mate. The females carry the sperm of the males in their bodies until the following spring.

Depending on the species, the pregnant female needs at least 40 days and as long as half a year to give birth to one offspring called a "pup." At birth, the pup will weigh about 25% of its mother's body weight.

The pup's mother will feed it her own milk, which is one of the characteristics of mammals compared to other animals. The communities of mothers and pups stay separate from the male bats and mothers will cooperate in taking care of their offspring until they are old enough to be independent.

A NEW BORN BAT

WHAT IS ECHOLOCATION?

Some bats see at night with extra-large eyes. However, some don't have very good eyesight and they use a different system to "see." It's called echolocation. Bats emit sounds from their larynxes through their mouths. It's fortunate for us that most of these sounds are too high-pitched for human ears to detect.

Bats can make sounds that scientists believe are like piercing screams that register at 140 decibels. The waves of sound bounce off the object they are hunting so they can determine its size and location. They can use echolocation for insects that are up to 5 meters away.

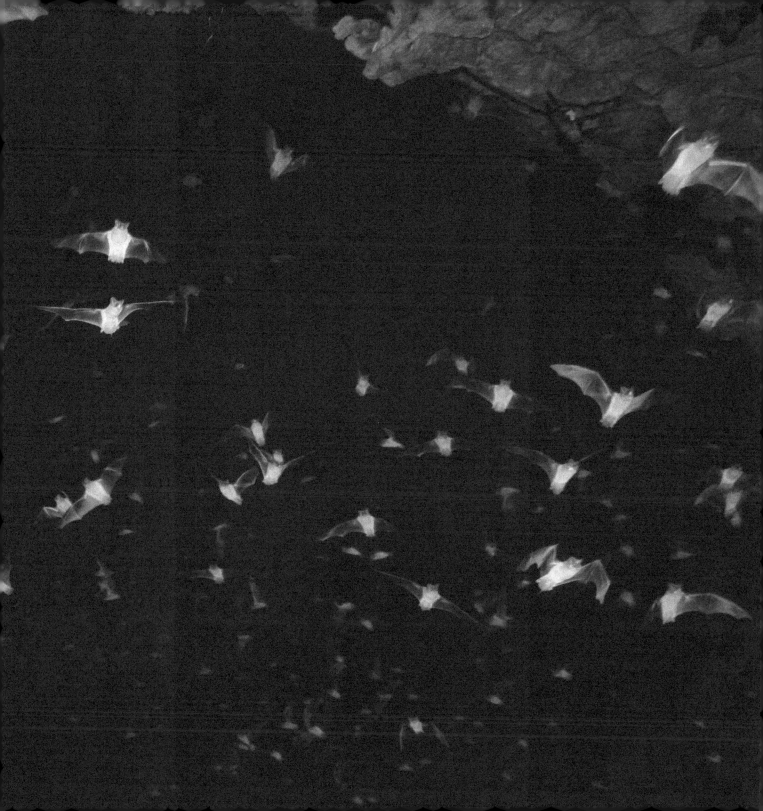

As a bat gets closer and closer to its prey, it intensifies its calls so it can pinpoint the insect's exact location. They can avoid wires or other obstacles that are as thin as a human hair. Bats that use echolocation, also called bio sonar, can hunt in complete darkness.

WHY ARE BATS IMPORTANT?

Bats are very important to environments all around the world. Over 500 species of plants are pollinated by bats and some species depend solely on bats. Cocoa, mango, and banana plants are all pollinated by bats. When bats pollinate plants, it's called chiropterophily. Plants that bats pollinate generally have pale-looking nocturnal blooms unlike the brightly colored daytime flowers favored by bees.

Pollination is only one aspect of the environment where bats are important. Bats also keep the populations of dangerous insects in check as well.

THE CONSERVATION STATUS OF BATS

Unfortunately, over 200 species of bats worldwide are in various stages of becoming endangered. The most endangered is Bulmer's fruit bat. Its sole habitat is one cave in New Guinea and there are only about 160 bats left. Over the last few years a terrible fungus described as "white-nose syndrome" has killed thousands of bats in North America. It's a white fungus that looks like powder and coats the muzzles, wings, and ears of the bats, attacking their bodies and weakening them.

IN REALITY..

Many people are scared of bats, but bats are fascinating creatures and, for the most part, they are harmless to humans.

In fact, they are extremely beneficial to people because they eat dangerous and harmful insects and pollinate plants. They are the only flying mammals and they range in size to having wingspans as wide as 6 feet to as small as just a few inches.

Awesome! Now that you've read about bats may want to read about more animals in the Baby Professor book Intelligent Animals You Need to Meet.

Visit

BABY PROFESSOR
EDUCATION KIDS

www.BabyProfessorBooks.com

to download Free Baby Professor eBooks
and view our catalog of new and exciting
Children's Books

CPSIA information can be obtained
at www.ICGtesting.com
Printed in the USA
LVHW062319240121
677394LV00056B/1761